The Amazing Book of BIRD RECORDS

The Largest, the Smallest, the Fastest, and Many More!

By Samuel G. Woods

Illustrations by Jeff Cline

BLACKBIRCH PRESS, INC.
WOODBRIDGE, CONNECTICUT

> For Nathan and Emma, may you both take flight one day.
> –SGW

Published by Blackbirch Press, Inc.
260 Amity Road
Woodbridge, CT 06525
web site: http://www.blackbirch.com
e-mail: staff@blackbirch.com

© 2000 Blackbirch Press, Inc.
First Edition

All rights reserved. No part of this book may be reproduced in any form without permission in writing from Blackbirch Press, Inc., except by a reviewer.

Printed in China

10 9 8 7 6 5 4 3 2 1

Photo Credits
Pages 5–6: ©Lior Rubin/Peter Arnold, Inc.; page 6 (inset): ©Kevin Schafer/Peter Arnold, Inc.; pages 6–7, 10–11, 12–13, 20–21, 24–25, 26 (inset), 30–31: ©Corel Corporation; pages 8–9: ©John R. MacGregor/Peter Arnold, Inc.; pages 14–15: ©Robert Maier/Animals Animals; Pages 16–17: ©PhotoDisc; pages 18–19: ©Robert A. Tyrell; pages 22–23: ©John Cancalosi/Peter Arnold, Inc.; page 27: ©Russell C. Hansen/Peter Arnold, Inc.; page 29: ©M. Seraillier.

Library of Congress Cataloging-in-Publication Data
Woods, Samuel G.
   The amazing book of bird records: the largest, the smallest, the fastest, and many more! / by Samuel G. Woods; illustrations by Jeff Cline.
   p. cm.
   Includes index.
   ISBN 1-56711-369-9
   1. Birds—Miscellanea—Juvenile literature. [1. Birds—Miscellanea. 2. Questions and answers.] I. Cline, Jeff, ill. II. Title

QL676.2.W66 2000
598—dc21   00-034304

Contents

The Longest-Lived 4

The Fastest Flying 6

Flies the Most 8

The Largest Flightless 10

The Largest Wingspan 12

The Largest Flighted 14

The Largest Above-Ground Nest 16

The Smallest 18

The Fastest Swimmer 20

The Longest Bill 22

The Slowest Flying 24

Migrates the Farthest 26

The Longest Feathers 28

The Greatest Force 30

Glossary 32

For More Information 32

Index 32

What's the LONGEST-LIVED Bird?

The Andean Condor

Some Andean condors have been known to live more than 70 years!

Andean Condors are the largest birds of prey.

NOTEPAD

Condors are actually a species of vulture, which is a bird of prey. Other birds of prey are owls, eagles, hawks, and falcons. The Andean Condor is the largest of all the birds of prey in the world. It can grow up to 52 inches (132 cm) long, and can have a wingspan of more than 10 feet (3 m)!

What's the FASTEST FLYING Bird?

The Peregrine Falcon

The fastest peregrine falcon ever clocked reached a speed of 124 miles (200 km) per hour!

NOTEPAD

The peregrine falcon is a bird of prey, also called a raptor. That means it hunts other animals for food. The peregrine's ability to reach high speeds is one of its most deadly weapons. While hunting, it will circle high above its prey. Then, it will dive at great speed, surprising and killing its victim with the impact of its super-sharp talons. The peregrine's hunting ability is quite impressive—it is successful once in every three tries.

A peregrine's great speed is one of its most effective hunting weapons.

Which Bird FLIES THE MOST?

The Common Swift

On average, these birds fly about 135,000 miles (217,300 km) per year! One bird recorded a nonstop trip of 310,000 miles (498,900 km)!

Swifts only stop flying to sleep and nest.

NOTEPAD

Swifts are definitely the bird world's most frequent fliers! They do nearly everything while flying. They catch their food as the fly, they communicate with each other in flight—they even mate while in flight. In fact, these birds only stop flying to sleep and nest. Many species of swift actually use their saliva to build their nests. These nests are highly prized by humans and are very valuable.

What's the LARGEST FLIGHTLESS Bird?

The Ostrich

Ostriches have been known to stand up to 8 feet (2.4 m) tall and to weigh more than 300 pounds (136 kg)!

NOTEPAD

An ostrich may be too heavy to fly, but it sure can run! At full speed, this large bird can reach speeds of more than 40 miles (64 km) per hour. It can take huge strides of 12 to 15 feet (4-5 m). The ostrich also holds the record for largest and heaviest bird egg. An average egg weighs about 3 pounds (1kg) and has a volume equal to about 2 dozen chicken eggs!

Ostriches are the world's largest birds, and the ones that lay the heaviest eggs.

What's the Bird with the LARGEST WINGSPAN?

The Marabou Stork

The average wingspan of a full-grown marabou stork is more than 13 feet (4 m)!

Storks are large birds that are related to vultures.

NOTEPAD

Marabous are some of the largest storks around. A full-grown marabou stands about 5 feet (150 cm) tall and weighs about 20 pounds (9 kg). Because they are so large, these birds need to eat about 25 ounces (700 g) of food each day. Like their cousins, the vultures, storks will feed on dead and rotting animals. They will also use their long, strong beaks to break into termite mounds and feast on the insects inside.

What's the LARGEST FLIGHTED Bird?

The Kobi Bustard

A male Kobi bustard can grow to 3.5 feet (1 m) tall and can weigh about 46 pounds (20 kg)!

Bustards are large birds that need a lot of food for energy.

NOTEPAD

Bustards are large, heavy birds. For them, flying takes a lot of work. That's why they prefer to spend most of their time on the ground, searching for food. They eat seeds, flowers, and leaves, but they also like to hunt small animals. A bustard will chase down mice, small lizards—even baby birds. Bustards are generally good runners. Only if they can't outrun an enemy will they take flight.

Which Bird Builds the LARGEST ABOVE-GROUND NEST?

The Bald Eagle

Some bald eagle nests have measured 10 feet (3 m) wide, 20 feet (6 m) long, and have weighed about 5,500 pounds (2,500 kg)! That's the weight of nearly three cars!

NOTEPAD

Bald eagles are big, heavy birds that like to nest way up high. Their nests, called aeries, must be super strong and well built. Not only are bald eagles heavy, they are also one of the few birds that use their nests all year long. Each year, the birds bring new sticks and branches to enlarge or strengthen their aerie. After a few years of constant usage, an eagle nest gets quite heavy. One nest in Ohio was known to have been in constant use for about 35 years!

Bald eagles use their nests all year long, unlike most other birds.

What's the SMALLEST Bird?

The Bee Hummingbird

The body of a full-grown bee hummingbird is little more than 2 inches (5 cm) long—that's about the size of a bumblebee!

Unlike any other birds, hummingbirds can fly backwards and can hover in midair.

NOTEPAD

Hummingbirds are the world's most incredible fliers. In proportion to its body, a hummingbird's flying muscles are especially large. These muscles allow a hummingbird to flap its wings much faster than any other bird. At top speed, a hummingbird may flap its wings 200 times per second. They are also the only birds that can fly backwards and can hover, motionless, in midair.

Which Bird Is the FASTEST SWIMMER?

The Gentoo Penguin

At top speed, a gentoo penguin can swim about 17 miles (27 km) per hour!

Gentoo penguins live in the South Pole and swim in the icy waters of the Antarctic circle.

NOTEPAD

Like most other penguins, the gentoo is found only in the Antarctic—the South Pole region. The average gentoo weighs about 12 pounds (6 kg) and stands about 30 inches (75 cm) high. These birds spend most of their time out in the icy waters of the area. As they swim, gentoos will most often hunt for fish near the water's surface, although they have been known to dive down as far as 330 feet (101 m)!

What's the Bird with the LONGEST BILL?

The Australian Pelican

An adult Australian pelican's bill can grow longer than 181 inches (46 cm)!

NOTEPAD

On average, pelicans are some of the world's largest birds. Adults can weigh up to 33 pounds (15 kg) and can have wingspans of more than 10 feet (3 m). A pelican's super-long bill is most useful for spearing fish. Some species will dive from high in the air and spear fish in the water. Other pelicans prefer to hunt as a group. They form an open circle in the water and drive schools of fish into shallow areas where they can be easily seen and snatched.

A pelican's long bill is best suited to spearing fish.

What's the SLOWEST FLYING Bird?

The American Woodcock

Woodcocks fly at an average of only 5 miles (8 km) per hour, which is slower than many humans can walk!

Woodcocks are heavy for their size and don't like to fly too often.

NOTEPAD

Woodcocks prefer to spend most of their time in tall grasses, looking for insects, earthworms, and snails near bogs and swamps. Their especially sensitive bill is well suited for rooting in the earth and finding tasty morsels. At an average of about 11 inches (28 cm) long, the woodcock is heavy for its size. Because they don't like to fly very often, woodcocks make short, irregular flights and then drop suddenly to the ground.

What's the Bird that MIGRATES THE FARTHEST?

The Arctic Tern

In the spring, a female Arctic tern will fly from the South Pole to the North Pole. That's a total of nearly 25,000 miles (40,200 km)! In the fall, the same bird will fly back to the South Pole, completing a journey equal to flying around the world!

Terns use visual clues as landmarks on their long journeys.

NOTEPAD

Arctic terns travel mostly along coastlines. Many scientists believe this is how these birds use visual clues to find their way. A tern's journey is long and often dangerous. Storms and strong winds may blow them far out over the open ocean. Thick fog can cause them to lose their direction. As they migrate, terns will stop at the mouths of large rivers. There, they can feed on insects and dive for fish.

Which Bird Has the LONGEST FEATHERS?

The Phoenix Fowl

The feathers on the tail of a Phoenix fowl can reach a length of more than 34 feet (10.4 m)! That's nearly the length of half a tennis court!

The Phoenix fowl is really a close relative of the common chicken.

NOTEPAD

The Phoenix fowl is a relative of the common chicken. In fact, this kind of fowl is commonly referred to as an ornamental chicken. Of the long-tailed species, the Onagadori is the only one to achieve such dramatic tail length. Originally bred in Europe and America, the Phoenix fowl is most often found with breast colorings of black, white, red, gold, and silver. There have been other colors bred, but they are extremely rare.

Which Bird Hits with the GREATEST FORCE?

The Red-Headed Woodpecker

On average, a red-headed woodpecker's beak hits a tree at 13 miles (21 km) per hour, causing its head to snap back and stop with a force of 10 g. (Humans can only survive a force of 9 g for several seconds!).

A woodpecker's beak is a powerful drilling tool.

NOTEPAD

A red-headed woodpecker's beak is a very powerful drill. It can punch holes in tough tree bark and can create hollowed-out nests in remarkably little time. Most often, a woodpecker pecks at tree bark in search of insects and sap. Its extremely long, wormlike tongue is coated in a sticky mucus. When an opening has been pecked, the bird's tongue goes in and probes for food. As the tongue moves, insects get stuck to it and are pulled out to be eaten.

Glossary

Bird of prey—bird that hunts other animals for food.

Bogs—an area of wet, spongy land.

Hover—when a bird remains in one place in the air.

Irregular—something that doesn't follow a normal pattern.

Migrate—when birds fly away during a certain time of the year to live in another region or climate.

Mucus—a slimy fluid that coats and protects the inside of a living thing's mouth, nose, or throat.

Species—a group of animals that have similar features.

Strides—long steps.

Talons—the sharp claws of a bird of prey.

Wingspan—the distance between the outer tips of the wings of a bird.

For More Information

Books

Kops, Deborah. *Vultures* (Wild Birds of Prey). Woodbridge, CT: Blackbirch Marketing, 2000.

Potts, Steve. *The Bald Eagle*. Mankato, MN: Capstone Press, 1997.

Rauzon, Mark. *Hummingbirds* (First Book). Danbury, CT: Franklin Watts, Inc., 1997.

Wechsler, Doug. *Bizarre Birds*. Honesdale, PA: Boyds Mill Press, 1999.

Video

Amazing Birds of America (Questar, Inc.), 1999.

Web Site

Bird of the Week
Learn about and listen to a different bird each week—www.birds.cornell.edu/bow

Peterson Online
Identify and read more about birds you see in your backyard—www.petersononline.com

Index

American woodcock, 24, 25
Andean condor, 4, 5
Antarctic, 21
Arctic tern, 26, 27
Australian pelican, 22

Bald eagle, 16, 17
Bee hummingbird, 18, 19
Bill, 22, 23, 25
Bird of prey, 5, 7

Bustards, 15

Chicken, 11, 29
Common swift, 8

Egg, 11

Feathers, 28
Flying, 6, 8, 9, 15, 19, 24, 26

Gentoo penguin, 20, 21

Hunt, 7, 15, 21, 23

Kobi, 14

Marabou stork, 12, 13

Nests, 9, 16, 17, 31

Ostrich, 10, 11

Pelicans, 23
Peregrine Falcon, 6, 7

Phoenix fowl, 28, 29

Raptor, 7
Red-headed woodpecker, 30, 31

Swifts, 9
Swim, 20, 21

Vulture, 5, 13

Wingspan, 5, 12, 23